£4-50
ARC
17/21

A WILTSHIRE LANDSCAPE

Scenes from the Countryside
1920-1940

A WILTSHIRE LANDSCAPE

Scenes from the Countryside
1920-1940

PHOTOGRAPHS FROM
A COLLECTION OWNED BY THE
WILTSHIRE BRANCH, C.P.R.E.

Text by Michael Marshman

PUBLISHED JOINTLY BY
COUNTRYSIDE BOOKS
AND
COUNCIL FOR THE PROTECTION OF
RURAL ENGLAND
WILTSHIRE BRANCH

First Published 1984
© Photographs: Council for the Protection
of Rural England
Wiltshire Branch 1984
© Text: Michael Marshman 1984

ISBN 0 905392 36 1

Designed by Mon Mohan/Jo Angell

Produced through MRM (Print Consultants) Ltd,
Baughurst, Hants.
Printed in England by Adams and Sons, Hereford.

Foreword

ENGLAND'S countryside is part of our national heritage. It contains the living history of our land. Fifty-seven years ago the Council for the Protection of Rural England was brought into being to protect the English landscape from the ravages of unplanned development and the destruction of irreplaceable features of our countryside.

On 11th May 1932, in the Town Hall, Trowbridge, 10 men met to form the first Executive Committee of the Wiltshire Branch of the Council for the Protection of Rural England. One of the men present at that meeting was Mr. Rivers Pollock, a gentleman extremely interested in amateur photography.

During the early years of its existence, photography played a major part in the activities of the Branch. Annual photographic competitions were organised and indeed, Mr. Cecil Beaton was approached to judge the competition one year, though was later called away to America and could not, in the event, judge the entries.

In 1937, the Branch Minute Book records that Miss Wardale, the local secretary, spoke to a committee meeting and 'referred to correspondence in the *Times,* advocating a photographic record of villages ..... the Committee considered it very desirable that such a record should be made in view of the rapid disappearance of characteristic features .... Mr. Pollock was invited to go into the matter'.

It appears from the old Minute Book and Annual Reports of the time, that the Committee continued to work on this project, until, unfortunately, the Second World War intervened, and the Branch records were discontinued during the period of the war. I could then find no further references in the documents until 1946, when the Branch Annual Report records that .. 'a small cabinet of slides of Mr. Pollocks is available at the CPRE office' and that 'the collection of photographs belonging to the late Mr. Pollock were lodged by his son' ..... 'for the especial benefit of the CPRE'.

We believe that the glass lantern slides were probably used to give occasional talks for some years after the war, until the Branch office was moved from its original location in Salisbury to its present room in Devizes. The old cabinet of slides was also moved to Devizes, but largely due to changes in committee members and branch personnel they were forgotten and remained untouched for at least 20 years, a fact which contributed to the unique condition in which they were found when I re-discovered them in 1982.

Mr. Pollock's son, Dr. Martin Pollock, now lives in Dorset but I was able to trace him and obtain his assurance that the slides had been a gift to the Branch, and I hope that he finds this book a permanent record which justifies the aims of his father and the other founding members of the Wiltshire Branch C.P.R.E., in making a photographic record of the Wiltshire countryside.

Susanne Preece
Wiltshire Branch, C.P.R.E.
St. Joseph's Place, Devizes

Acknowledgements

ON BEHALF of the Wiltshire Branch of the Council for the Protection of Rural England, our particular thanks go to the late Mr. Rivers Pollock, a founder member of the Branch, and to his son, Dr. Martin Pollock, who, in 1946, gave the cabinet of glass lantern slides to the Wiltshire Branch C.P.R.E., so making this record of the Wiltshire countryside possible.

Thanks also go to Michael Marshman for writing the text and captions and for his invaluable help and enthusiam in compiling the book. Also a special word of thanks to Lesley Marshman, for all the help she has given in its preparation.

Our very grateful thanks go to Roy Purton and to his company Acculith, for carrying out the conversion work on the glass slides, and for producing the negatives for these photographs. I know that the work took rather longer than was originally anticipated because the staff at Acculith found the pictures so interesting, and I trust this did not disrupt the smooth running of his company too much.

To Ken Rogers, our thanks for his valuable help with archive research.

To Pamela Coleman and Paul Robinson of Devizes Museum, our thanks for the advice they gave in the beginning, when I first looked at the slides.

To Nicholas and Suzanne Battle, our appreciation for their keen interest in the photographic collection and their support in publishing this unique story of scenes from our Wiltshire heritage.

Finally, a special word of thanks to my husband, Roy Preece, for his patience during the past 12 months, while I have been overseeing this project, and for the help he gave me with some particular arrangements.

Contents

Introduction

Although the inter war period is very recent history the increasingly frequent changes wrought by modern technology give to it a feeling that is several lifetimes removed from the 1980s. Up to that time changes in the rural landscape had lagged far behind those of town and industry and to a large extent it was the impetus given by two World Wars that created a heavier investment in machinery on the farm and a corresponding fall in the number of people who obtained their living from the land. Many of the people pictured in this book worked the land in the 19th century and would have known much harsher conditions, lower wages and a poorer standard of living.

In many ways Wiltshire was a backwater. It had no heavy industry; its chief manufacture, that of woollen cloth in the towns of the west of the county, was in decline and the only industrial centre was the works of the Great Western Railway at Swindon. Apart from Swindon and the cathedral city of Salisbury, most people lived in medium sized market towns such as Trowbridge, Chippenham, Devizes and Warminster or smaller ones such as Marlborough and Wilton. Many industries were based on farming, malting, flour milling, dairy products and meat processing, and so directly or indirectly far more people earned their living from farming in the 1920s and 30s than is the case today.

Wiltshire is divided into the higher areas of chalk and the lower vales of clay and greensand. This topographical division is reflected in different methods of farming, ways of thinking and sometimes even forms of speech. The upland areas are Salisbury Plain, which throughout the 20th century has gradually been taken over by the War Department, and the Marlborough Downs, whose racehorse gallops have to some extent replaced the sheep runs. In the vales the fields and farms are smaller and the villages lie closer together, while all the towns were served by good lines of communication via canal, railway and road. The lower lands were once extensively wooded with hedgerow timber but, with the destruction of the elm, the countryside now presents a far more open appearance than was the case 50 years ago.

Although these pictures are of rural life it must be remembered that there were very close links between town and country. The market towns acted as clearing houses for the produce of their dependent villages and farms while the countryman's purchases of household furniture and equipment, clothes and agricultural machinery came from the town. Many townspeople themselves were only one or two generations removed from the rural life and several returned in the summer to assist with haymaking. People living in either town or country would have many friends and relatives in the other and the sharp distinctions that differentiate life in the big towns and cities from the country were almost non existent in Wiltshire. Today we have grown much further away from rural life over the last 50 years. Despite the fact that most families can travel wherever they wish in England the townsman is far less in sympathy with the country than he was two generations ago.

Not all facets of country life and farming practices are illustrated here. This is the photographic collection of a Society that was concerned both to preserve a record of a way of life that was nearing its end and to ensure the protection of the countryside against increasing urbanization. Old photographs, like old memories, rarely dwell on the unpleasant parts of life: what is recalled are the happy occasions, the sunny days, the successful harvests and the outings and fun. While the bad days and the struggles to bring up a family on little money lie dormant it is only fair to remember that the ordinary times, that were neither good nor bad, which made up by far the greater part of the year, are also often forgotten.

I have used these photographs to illustrate a way of life for which I have a great affection, even though I was not born until after the Second World War and therefore saw only a few vestiges of this era of rural England in the 1950s. Rather than give detailed descriptions of what can be seen, or the histories of some of the people, I have tried to give an impression of what life was like in a period when machines did not dominate most of men's actions and there was more time and space in life. After all, these excellent photographs can speak for themselves.

MICHAEL MARSHMAN
Trowbridge, July 1984

The Wiltshire Countryside

L IKE MOST rural landscapes that of Wiltshire has undergone dramatic changes during the last 40 to 50 years. The gradual process of hedge removal and field enlargement has accelerated into a breakneck gallop with whole areas of the countryside being denuded of hedges, spinneys and isolated mature trees. The paintings of Constable and Turner show a lush, verdant early 19th century England which the 20th century has forgotten, an England which is unlikely ever to be recaptured save in the imagination. That England would never be economic to modern farming values and indeed the good old days in rural England were often far from good for those who lived through them.

We can catch an echo of this rich greenness in photographs of the 1920s and 30s. On many farms the rate of work was still measured in genuine horsepower and the strength in the backs of horses and men provided the main energy for any changes. For this reason there were unlikely to be large scale alterations to the rural scene. There were still landowners and farmers who would pay a shilling for a good sapling left by a labourer when hedging, while many ponds, now infilled for reasons of piped water supply and good drainage, were fulfilling their old function as watering places for animals.

Laden haywains would trundle down deep leafy lanes with overhanging branches plucking a wispy tithe of the haysel. Substantial numbers of farmhands were required to work much of the land; mechanisation had gone some way to reducing their number but the large farms and machines which required few men to run them mostly belonged to an unimaginable post war era. In the villages, and many of the towns, the language spoken was Wiltshire, a dialect handed down in unbroken succession with no strident outside influences to change and 'improve' it. When Wiltshiremen had gone to fight in the Great War they took the speech of Wiltshire with them; by the time of the Second World War the dialect they carried through the world was only slightly less distinct but in the post war years the bludgeoning effects of radio and television and the desire to speak proper English and so avoid betraying one's rural background are killing off the familiar speech.

The focal point of rural life was the village. Changes there had been; the motor bus and car were replacing the carrier and pony trap; telephone, telegram and radio had brought instant information and news while the services of piped water, electricity and even mains sewerage had spread from nearby towns. But there were still some isolated villages where water came from the pump, cooking took place on a coal or wood burning range and artificial light was emitted from paraffin or oil lamps. Sewerage disposal was by the means of a cess pit and in most houses the only form of heating, apart from the kitchen range, was the open fire. Village life could still seem more important than that of the outside world and the exploits of the local poacher far more interesting to them than the entertainment based gossip of the present day is to us.

It is interesting to note how self sufficient many of these villages still were. Those close to a town had lost some shops and trades to urban competition while in the smaller communities lack of business had closed some of the firms that were flourishing in the 19th century. Sutton Veny, 3 miles from Warminster, had a population in 1931 of 533. There was a post office and stationers, a grocer and a baker while trades included a sweep, both a boot maker and a boot repairer, a plumber and a dressmaker. A smith and farrier had expanded into a motor engineer and haulage contractor while the village included a representative of that most useful species of country tradesmen, the general dealer.

Urchfont, where many of the photographs in this book were taken, is 5 miles from Devizes and in 1931 its population was 649. Being slightly larger and farther from a market town it could boast a general store, 2 drapers, a butcher, a baker, a grocer, a post office which included a general store and 3 other shops; 10 shops in all. Craftsmen included a blacksmith, a saddler, a carpenter, a chimney sweep and a clock repairer, while there was also a builder, a haulage contractor, saw mills, a garage and a motor bus company. A thriving busy village.

Even more self reliant was Great Bedwyn, 7 miles from Marlborough, with a population of 789. Here there were shops and trades to satisfy most everyday requirements. To bring you into the world there was a district nurse and medical officer; to clothe and shoe you, a draper and a bootmaker; to feed and provision you, a butcher, 2 grocers, a baker and 3 other stores. During your life you would need the services of the post office, the coal merchant, the blacksmith, the carpenter, the plumber, the newsagent and possibly the wheelwright, the motor engineer, the brickmaker and the man who hired out cars. If you received temperance visitors whom you could not take to either of the village pubs there was the Primrose Cafe; when you were eventually laid to rest in the churchyard there was a well established monumental mason to carve and erect a memorial over you. In this community, and there were many like it, the trip to the local town could still be regarded as a small luxury rather than a necessary fact of rural life. When you did need to travel there were plenty of opportunities and Great Bedwyn railway station was on the London line.

Indeed at this time public transport was more readily available than at any other time before and with far better services than those of today. All towns, and most villages, had their railway station providing not only passenger transport but an important means of bringing in such items as stone, coal and brick. The produce of the area, milk, cattle, corn or wool, could also be carried away by the goods train. The railway had become part of the village; the station with its flower beds and allotments and the station master and porter taking their mid-day pint at the local inn. A way of life far removed from that of the heavy lorries that were to shatter, pollute and defile the peace of many a Wiltshire village in the following decades. On the road omnibuses provided transport to nearby towns while most villagers would enjoy at least one charabanc outing to the seaside each year. The spread of cheaper mass-produced cars was already beginning a transport revolution and by the 1920s most communities possessed a garage or motor engineer.

Much more frequently during this period were young people going to the towns to find work. Secondary education had necessitated some travel to town and wider horizons opened up before the eyes of the new generation than had been dreamed of by their predecessors. This, however, was a two way process and not just a drain on country resources; well educated young men and women, from college or school of agriculture, would often return to their village bringing with them new skills and knowledge. Sometimes town dwellers, tired of urban life, would move out and these too would enrich the countryside with different views, opinions and crafts.

This way of life, which could be both pleasant and hard, full of interest or of repetition, was drawing to a close. Up to now things had changed but slowly; gradually man was better housed, clothed, fed and entertained, but the way of life where the land and service to it were of prime importance continued. A farmer rarely bought land as an investment or looked upon his farm as a factory style business; both he and his labourers were servants of their acres and took pride in the condition of the land, the state of their crops and animals and getting jobs done at the proper time. The shadows of modern warfare and the harsh economic facts of life which were to be their consorts were to end this final flowering of a centuries old way of life; a remnant would still be there in the 1950s but it would soon be swept away.

▲ This view of Salisbury Plain, in the last days of its glory of sheep cropped turf, shows rolling acres of tough downland grasses which were dotted with the attractive small flowers of the chalk. Sheep had been the staple economy of the Plain for centuries but were fast disappearing in the 1920s and during the 1940s much of the land was ploughed when wartime necessity and chemical fertilisers combined to make the growing of corn viable. The villages of the Plain are most often strung along the valleys with the fields of each parish stretching some miles to the hill tops on both sides. A few villages, such as Chitterne and Tilshead, were lonely and isolated and had developed self contained communities that received only infrequent visitors.

▲ The most imposing feature of lowland Wiltshire was the elms; trees of parkland, field and hedgerow, they gave interest to the flat clay vales and in summer provided areas of refreshing coolness to both man and beast. Many roads were lined with elms which hid farms and villages from view until the traveller was upon them. Now, when a whole village can be seen from some distance, it becomes difficult to remember that not many years ago the only hint that an approaching visitor received of a village was an embosked steeple and a few chimneys with a haze of smoke from domestic fires. These elms at Blacklands Farm, Rainscombe, were set in verdant parkland sheltered in a deep bay in the hills behind Oare. Within the space of a few years the ravages of Dutch Elm disease destroyed most of the trees which made up the pattern of countryside familiar to those who lived in the years before the Second World War. With modern farming methods it is unlikely that we shall ever see Wiltshire looking the same again even though some disease resistant elms will come back. The county is a great deal poorer for the passing of these great trees.

▲ Until recent times Wiltshire chalkland streams were used to irrigate fields during the winter. The flowing waters would deposit sediment and nutrients while protecting the growing grass against frost. According to John Aubrey this system began at Wylye in about 1635 and had spread north east to the river Kennet by 1646. Water was led from the stream to the head of the meadow and conducted in a grid of ditches across the land. When this was operating the pasture was covered by an inch of gently flowing water which was channelled back in the stream at the lower end of the meadow. This drowning of the meadows began in December when the hatches were opened and was continued until March. By then the farmer had an early bite of spring grass at least 4 weeks before other farmers who did not possess water meadows. Flooding these meadows was an expert job and the countrymen who practised it, called drowners, passed on their skills by word of mouth and were often scornful of the prowess of younger men. With the virtual disappearance of sheep from many parts of Wiltshire around 1930 the drowners with their craft passed into other farming jobs or retired and the water meadows became derelict. Today many of them have unfortunately been ploughed out but in some the remains of parallel ditches, about 5 yards apart, or a broken wooden hatch serve as mute reminders of farming ways before the general use of chemical fertilisers.

◀ On Salisbury Plain the only downland valley with a permanent stream providing a rarely failing source of water for animals and irrigation is that of the river Till. The other valleys contain winterbournes with streams flowing only in the wetter months. The Till rises on the Plain between Shrewton and Orcheston but in times of high rainfall springs rise at Tilshead giving the river another 3 to 4 miles of extra length. The river passes through Winterbourne Stoke and Berwick St. James before joining the Wylye at Stapleford. This summer scene shows a traditional picture of cattle standing in the cooling water while grazing on the riverside herbage.

▲ Savernake Forest covers a large area to the east of Marlborough and was the only forest to be the property of a subject rather than the monarch. After medieval times, when it had been governed by strict forest laws, the estate was landscaped during the 18th century and laid out in segments, separated by rides, entered by an impressive Grand Avenue of beech and elm. the Wardenship of Savernake has remained in the same family since the Norman Conquest; the present Marquess of Ailesbury being descended from the original Norman owner, Richard Esturmy. The forest was managed by the owners until the late 1930s when the Forestry Commission was granted a 999 year lease with limits imposed on the quantity of softwoods that could be planted. Deer, nowadays mainly fallow and roe with only a few red, have been in the forest throughout the Wardenship and not too many years ago were still providing a strong temptation to poachers, especially during times of low wages and high unemployment.

▲ Grovely is an ancient forest, somewhat reduced in size, set on a ridge between the valleys of the Wylye and the Nadder as can be seen on the horizon of this picture. In this view, taken from near Stapleford, long strip lynchetts can be seen on the lower slopes indicating the extent of medieval cultivation of marginal land during times of population expansion. Near Grovely Wood, and closely associated with it, lies the village of Great Wishford. On Oak Apple Day (May 29th) celebrations take place which could well be surviving remnants of prehistoric festivals of the forest. Early in the morning every villager walks up the hill to Grovely Wood and cuts some of the growing green wood. Houses and church are then decorated with the boughs while a party of villagers travel to Salisbury to lay an offering of oak branches in front of the cathedral altar. Even the casual visitor may catch a distant echo of a once powerful message concerning the renewal and rising of the life force through the burgeoning greenwood. The well known shout of 'Grovely, Grovely, and all Grovely' is followed by dancing outside the cathedral and a village fete in the afternoon.

17

◀ Set in a shallow valley on the Marlborough Downs the dignified village of Aldbourne gives an impression of quietness despite the bustle of the Swindon to Hungerford Road which it straddles. Sheep built up the prosperity of this village but in the 17th and 18th centuries the specialist craft of bell founding grew up among a few local families. The village is set around a fine green with a Perpendicular church at the highest point, many pleasant cottages and houses dating back to the 16th century and the Blue Boar Inn which is probably contemporary with the church. This view from the Ogbourne Road shows a rickyard behind its farm and thatched barn.

▲ The Wylye is a splendid chalk stream flowing clear and sweet and is much loved by fishermen. Rising near Warminster it flows south east through very pleasant fields and villages, being joined at Wilton by the Nadder, and then entering the Avon at Salisbury. The best way to enjoy the river is to leave the main Salisbury road one mile south east of Warminster and take the turning to Sutton Veny. You then travel the southern bank along what must be one of the most attractive roads in all Wiltshire, coming to Wilton through Ditchampton, once the home of the Wiltshire farmer, writer and broadcaster, A.G. Street. The mellow villages and rich pastures have been little changed over the last 50 years although far less of the inhabitants of the former now get their living from the latter. The river is seen here at Great Wishford where it swings to the east around the village before continuing to South Newton.

▲ Timber had been an important agricultural crop from medieval times and woodlands were efficiently managed and coppiced. By the 20th century much had fallen into neglect but some notable forests remained and a few had become part of large country house estates. From the 18th century the most memorable feature of Savernake Forest had been the Grand Avenue. The 29th Warden of Savernake Forest, the Marquess of Ailesbury, tell us in his book, *The Wardens of Savernake Forest* (1949), that this work was begun by Charles, Lord Bruce, who was the first man to plant extensive beech avenues there. The trees were placed close together on either side of narrow tracks, as can be seen. Thus the trees slowly grew to a height of over 90 feet with no low branches except on the outside of the avenues. Later the advice of Capability Brown was sought and he provided a long essay containing ideas generated on several visits. Most of these ideas were taken up and vistas opened by selective tree felling. The Grand Avenue itself gives an impressive view from Tottenham House, former home of the Ailesburys, to a tall stone column erected on the occasion of King George III's restoration to health in 1781.

▲ The Vale of Pewsey, lying between the Marlborough Downs to the north and Salisbury Plain to the south, is about 12 miles in length. Even today, standing on Knap Hill, one can see few signs of human habitation, just a glimpse of farm, church or small village amid neatly hedged fields and small copses. The villages of the Vale are quiet and secretive places, little known even to Wiltshire folk. Here is some of the richest farming in the south of England with fertile greensand on gault clay sandwiched by upland chalk.

The farms have always been prosperous and huge fairs for both cattle and sheep were held on the nearby hills. One such was on Tan Hill, to the north, on August 5th every year. One of the highest points in the county is here, Milk Hill at 964 feet above sea level. Several small tumps rise within the Vale to heights of over 600 feet; one such is Etchilhampton Hill seen here from Urchfont Manor across the typical Vale landscape of pasture and trees.

▲ In the inter-war years the English countryside was undergoing transformation. This view of West Lavington in 1930 shows some of the results. A wooden pylon brings power cables into the village to provide electricity to both farmstead and cottage while a profusion of telegraph poles indicates that not only the post office, rectory and big house have a telephone but several smaller homes and farms too. The proliferation of telephones in some villages did destroy one regular social call, when the village gossips would look in at the post office 'just to have a read of the telegrams'. Another new feature in the village in the 1920s and 30s was the council houses which enabled a farm labourer to be independent of his employer and the tied cottage system. These also introduced the countryman to a higher standard of living than was possible in a centuries old and picturesque but completely unmodernised and thoroughly inconvenient cottage.

◄ From earliest times Wiltshiremen must have been conscious of the works of their forebears, even if at times these were ascribed to giants, wizards or the devil. Nowhere is there such a sense of present day life co-existing with the distant past than at Avebury. The traditional village is built within a late Neolithic henge monument, which is both earlier and greater than Stonehenge, and split by the Devizes to Swindon Road which brings hordes of visitors to gaze, often uncomprehendingly, at the glorous achievements of a vanished race. It was between 1925 and 1939 that Alexander Keiller excavated Avebury and re-erected many of the stones. Local men were employed under the expert direction of the archaeologists and would have learned more than they thought possible of their county's prehistory.

The first picture shows one of the smaller stones of the Circle which has been excavated and reset. The second scene presents a general view of the excavations on the Swindon road. Techniques of modern archaeology, pioneered in south Wiltshire by General Pitt Rivers are in evidence, though few present day excavations have the spoil removed by horse and cart. The stone to the right can be seen in close up in the third picture. This shows a detailed examination of a standing stone to determine dating and method of erection. The stone is well propped with baulks of timber to prevent a similar accident to one in the 14th century when a barber surgeon was crushed beneath a stone that was probably being toppled and broken up for building material; his skeleton is in Avebury Museum which contains most of the finds from this important site. The bungalow on the left hand side of the road in the second picture has been removed in the 1930s as part of a scheme to take away all houses from within the circle. In 1937 Marlborough Rural District Council started building houses at nearby Avebury Trusloe and later decided to rehouse all Avebury residents there. Fortunately this plan seems to have been forgotten and the houses, many of which were built from the standing stones, remain.

The Farming Year

WILTSHIRE farming had traditionally relied on sheep, and later grain, on the chalklands, and dairying, pigs and poultry in the clay vales with a scattering of market gardens and orchards on the greensand between the two. Sheep normally spent the summer and autumn on the downs and during the winter were folded in the lower fields. In spring the lambs, and later the ewes, would get the first bite of grass from the water meadows. Grain comprised wheat, barley and oats, varying in acreage from year to year with barley decreasing in proportion to wheat and oats becoming more popular as being the most prolific crop and least costly to produce.

In general the upland farms tended to be medium to large in size while those of the vales were small to medium sized. Dairying was the main occupation of the latter with much milk sent to London and substantial quantities being turned into butter and cheese at factories in the local towns. Although Wiltshire once had its own distinctive cheese there was very little of it made in the farmhouse at this time nor was there much home produced cream or butter. Waste products from dairying were used to help fatten the pigs which were a feature of the mixed farming economy. Wiltshire bacon and ham were well known and factories such as Harris of Calne and Bowyers of Trowbridge took much of the output of the local pig production. Poultry farming on a large scale was not very common but most farms had a flock of free range hens, ducks or geese which provided fresh eggs to the people of local towns.

During the years between the wars farm mechanisation made some progress and although not shown in these photographs many petrol driven tractors and even some steam powered vehicles were in use on the farms. Often, however, the capital outlay on such equipment caused much serious thought before any investment was made and most farmers, especially the smaller ones preferred to rely on old fashioned horse power. The chief improvement in machinery came with the spread of more efficient binders, reapers, cultivators and seed drills. A change in farming practice which was to have long-lasting effects was the increased use of artificial fertilisers. Prior to this time land enrichment had been brought about either by pasturing animals on the fields, spreading the contents of the farmyard dungheap over the land or spraying slurry from the pig styes. From the 1920s corn growing began to depend more and more on specialised artificial fertilisers, eventually these developed to such an extent as to allow the ploughing of downland which could never naturally support continuous crops of corn.

The changes in farming at this period were widespread. Unprofitable corn prices had led to an increase in milk production which by use of the Hosier bail system of milking, a Wiltshire invention, led to many fields that were remote from the farmyard becoming available for dairy cattle. One of these bail systems complete would cost about £300 and with spring heifers at between £15 and £18 each it was reasonably inexpensive to set up a milking herd of 70 cows on a farm of 250 to 300 acres. By 1939 the popularity of dairying had led to 46% of farm income in the chalk valleys coming from milk and over 54% in the clay vales. Sheep virtually disappeared from their traditional areas on Salisbury Plain and in consequence this led to a drop in the acreage of root vegetables on which the sheep had been folded. With increases in both dairy and beef cattle, however, there was a corresponding increase in the acreages given over to kale and other greenstuffs used as cattle feed. For economic rather than technical reasons the water meadows were falling into disuse for although the idea and mechanics of producing early grass this way were superb the high cost in terms of labour needed to maintain them forced many farmers to leave their river meadows dry.

After the good profitable years of the Great War, when home grown foodstuffs were in great demand and farmers became wealthy, agriculture sank back into a depressed state and many farmers who continued their style of life as before ended up owing money to their bank and in some cases losing their farm. Agricultural wages had risen from 20 shillings a week in 1917 to a peak of 46 shillings in 1920 but with the abolition of wage fixing in 1921 this dropped back to 30 shillings a week. This fall was not quite as catastrophic as it sounds as with the general economic depression there was a corresponding fall in prices. By 1939 wages has risen to 38 shillings but there were less men in employment on the land. During the early years of the 20th century farmers had found that their farms were more cost effective if they employed fewer men at higher wages than if they had large numbers of poorly paid workers as had been the practice of their Victorian parents and grandparents.

More farmers were buying their own farms and during the 1920s and 30s there was quite an increase in the number of owner farmers. Landlords were finding that for taxation and other reasons the letting of farmland was becoming unprofitable and farmers, who had made money during the war, and young men, with the aid of bank loans, were able to purchase their own land. An attitude that characterised both farmers and labourers was their love of the land whether they owned it or not. This showed itself in the way the countryman would often put the needs of the land before himself; a farmer who was leaving his land at Michaelmas would cultivate it as carefully as ever even though someone else would reap the benefits; a farmhand would sometimes work unpaid overtime to finish a job he was not satisfied with. A pride in their work and in their farm showed through at a time when men did not consider themselves masters of the land but its custodians, caring for it so that it was passed on in good heart to the next generation. In his lifetime a man would see a score of good seasons, a score of bad and a lot of middling ones. Over the years it averaged itself out and a farm would provide a reasonable living.

This period saw the beginning of the end for many families that had been farming for generations. At the outbreak of hostilities in 1914, the farmers' sons were not slow in joining up; they who had fearlessly ridden to hounds and taken part in steeplechases, now took their horses to France, while others who, as boys, had learned to shoot rabbits and pheasants now turned their sights to human targets. Many fell and remained in France and so failed to inherit the farms which were their birthright. Whole farming families had been wiped out in this way and when time came for the father to retire, the farm was sold and the basis of a new farming dynasty began.

Those sons who did come back, or those too young for the war, learned new practices at agricultural college to add to the knowledge already gained on their fathers' farms. Sometimes these young men would take a small farm to learn the hard economies of farming or, if the family farm were large enough, would take over responsibility for the management of part of their father's operations.

These changes to the old order occurred gradually and did not apparently indicate the great alteration to farming practices that was to come. Agriculture had always suffered depressions, which often brought about some new methods, but never before had it to face the sort of challenge that was to be issued by World War II. We can see now that it was this event rather than the Great War which totally changed the face of English farming and removed the horse completely. Doubtless, the changes would have taken place in time but not so rapidly.

Backend

THE BACKEND of the year traditionally began with the ploughing after the last of the harvest was in. The stubble fields were turned into gleaming brown furrows to await the action of the frosts to help break down the earth. Ploughing was by horse, tractor, or occasionally, even as late as 1940, by steam. If winter wheat, which could have a yield up to 25% greater than its spring sown counterpart, or oats were to be sown harrowing, rolling and drilling would also take place. It was the season for tidying the land. Hedges would be cut and laid and hazes of blue smoke would indicate where trimmings and weeds were being burned. In readiness for the rains of winter ditches were cleared so that water was carried swiftly away and would not cause waterlogging of the fields preventing early cultivation in the spring.

After the rich feeding of the previous spring and summer, fatstock and unwanted animals were sent to market and a considerable amount of time could be spent in buying and selling beasts. Most country towns had retained their markets, some specialising in cattle, sheep or grain and others acting as general markets. This was also the time of the fairs, remnants of the hiring or mop fairs when workers were engaged for the year, but now giving themselves entirely over to pleasure and bringing roundabouts, helter skelters, animal shows and boxing booths to country dweller and townsman alike. These fairs provided a great beacon of colour in what was becoming the grey time of the year.

For the leaves were beginning to fall and in the pub two phrases, 'the nights be drawin' in' and 'tis the time of the year comin' on' would bring a reminder of the harder life in centuries past when this season caused apprehension of great hardships and perhaps even death. Even in the 20th century the winter was a hard time and a squirrel like mentality persisted as stocks of coal and wood for domestic use and hay, roots and other animal foodstuffs on the farm were built up and hoarded.

This was the beginning of that part of the year when the countrymen had a little time to engage in sport. Hunting was enjoyed by both farmer and labourer although the former was on his hunter among the gentry and the latter followed hounds on foot. Shooting of both pheasants and partridges was for the wealthy although the poorer man was able to bag rabbits or pigeons and occasionally, when undetected, a hare or carefully preserved game bird. Fishing was open to all and although the trout of the chalk streams were jealously guarded by keepers and water bailiffs, many families did not despise the muddier flavour of coarse fish while eels always made a welcome dish when the first frosts were about.

As Christmas approached, the countryside had the appearance of an animal about to go into hibernation. Everything had been tidied up and was slowing down; both field and woodland were to be left for two to three months largely unattended while life contracted into farmyard and village. Horses and cattle were brought into stables, barns or home pastures while sheep were brought down to the lower fields of root crops. Wind, frost, snow and rain could do their worst, the countryside was prepared.

▲ The vastness of the ploughman's task is apparent from this picture taken below Goose Hill at Urchfont. During a day's ploughing a man would walk between 8 and 10 miles in turning over one acre while maintaining a straight furrow and holding the plough steady despite the obstructions of buried stones or roots. Back breaking, arm aching work, plodding through heavy sticky soil which clung to the boots adding extra pounds to be picked up at every step. The old ploughmen used to drink many pints of cider during the day to 'put back' what they lost, yet their furrow was as straight at the end of the day as at the beginning. Great pride was taken in ploughing and on Sunday afternoons ploughmen would often walk to neighbouring farms to see the standard of another's work. Ploughing matches were frequently held and local champions held in great respect, being often better known than the farmer for whom they worked.

▲ The management of a team of horses required great skill and the horseman, who was responsible for ploughing, harrowing and rolling, was regarded as one of the most important workers on the farm. The care of the horse was paramount; the team were fed and groomed before dawn and at the mid-morning break they were not allowed to stand still for too long in case they caught a chill; at noon they were unhitched and taken back to the stable to be fed and watered; they then worked through the afternoon until dusk when the ploughman fed and groomed them before he had his own supper. Often one horse had to be replaced and a youngster would be stabled and worked with an older horse who would teach him the job. To work as a team horses had to be both compatible and companionable; selection of the right pair was an important business. Ploughing had started as soon as the corn harvest was in and the ricks thatched. It was important to plough as much land as possible before the hard frosts got into the ground and made the task very difficult, if not impossible. This team at Potterne Wick were doing just that late in 1931.

▲ An important part of village economy was still the cottager's pig. This would be fed on household scraps and vegetable matter from the garden, supplemented with a few pig nuts begged or bought from a local farmer. Often 2 pigs were kept and the meat from one would pay for foodstuffs, the fee of the local butcher and 2 replacement piglets to be fattened up to nine score baconers. Home cured bacon and ham from the second pig would provide several months' supply for a family, while the fat was rendered down for lard. For a few old countrymen this latter, in company with bread and raw onions, provided a satisfying meal, washed down with beer or cider at mid-day. This sow, 'Lodger', a Wessex Saddleback, had no such immediate fate awaiting her. Saddlebacks are a tough breed and have good mothering qualities which makes them an important part of cross-breeding programmes on the farm. A good sow such as this will rear 2 litters of up to 10 piglets each every year, although at this moment Lodger seems more interested in where her next meal is coming from than in future offspring.

▲ Market was an important part of farming life, not only as an opportunity for buying and selling but as a social occasion when you could meet your fellow farmers and discuss such matters as harvest prospects, new machinery and the iniquities of the Ministry of Agriculture. This picture comes from Devizes' Monday Market Street, now somewhat altered, and shows the auctioneer's booth beyond the cattle pens. An interesting detail is the hurdles which have been placed across the lower part of the ground floor windows of the Castle Hotel to prevent damage by inquisitive or frightened beasts. The hotels and inns provided a special lunch called a Market Ordinary or Farmer's Ordinary and licensing hours were extended into the afternoon, as is still the case in some Wiltshire towns. There was a protocol in where a man ate and drank on these occasions; the farmers tended to frequent the best hotel while their sons used another, the dealers, drovers and farm labourers went to different inns and pubs. In Wiltshire dialect there is a word 'peart' meaning lively but in some parts of the county on market days farmers gave it another meaning; a man described as 'market peart' was to be left alone to his own devices; often after initial liveliness during the day, on the journey home the horse had to find his own way while his master drowsed in the trap. This state of affairs was one of many changed by the spread of the internal combustion engine.

▲ Small branches from felled trees were lopped off and bundled into faggots to be used to fire bake ovens. Here a load is being transported at Woodbridge Mill, Littleton Pannell. The remaining trunk of the tree would often lie for up to a year in the open air before being taken to the saw mill. The standing timber on a farm could be a valuable asset which in hard times a farmer might have to sell; on a change of ownership the incoming man sometimes found it necessary to sell the living timber immediately in order to pay back some of the loan from his bank.

▲ The famous Cherhill Tithe Barn, demolished in 1956, was 110 feet long with side aisles. The large roof was composed of stone slates and the whole provided an impressive structure in a small village. Unfortunately the 20th century had little use for these large barns where the harvest was once carried in on great wagons and stacked high inside. A good harvest then ensured winter work for the men who would thresh the grain by hand while the wind blowing through the two opposing great doors would winnow it. Machine threshing changed the barns into stores for hay, animal feeds and farm implements, often in quantities which were dwarfed by the immensity of the old buildings.

▲ When threshing had been done by hand during the winter months the grain was afterwards stored in barns set on staddle stones to prevent rats and mice gaining access. By the 20th century these only remained as charming redundant survivors that were perhaps used for occasional storage. This pair at West Kennet were falling into disrepair in the 1920s but similar ones from Longleat and Great Chalfield can be seen in the Museum of Lackham College of Agriculture near Lacock.

◄ At this time of year and through the winter months the farmyard was a scene of great activity. Cattle were often overwintered here being fed on concentrates, hay and roots; the resultant muck heap being spread over the land to increase fertility at no additional cost save that of labour. To a townsman's eye the farmyard must have seemed an untidy place; there were often piles of machinery, timber or abandoned household articles; liquid seeped out of the midden; a smell that was sharp, strong and ammoniac hung in the air while both cats and hens prowled among the barns. This scene at Urchfont Manor Farm is more orderly although broken gates, awaiting repair, lean against the fence and feeding troughs are scattered in the yard. What appears to be a clamp of root crops for winter feed is in the corner.

▲ To be a carter was a proud calling; working with horses, having a fine turn out and at times riding when others walked. Maurice Ferris was a carter at Urchfont and is pictured in 1933. The jobs of a carter varied from season to season but at this time of year he was likely to be carrying green vegetable matter to the stockyard to feed the cattle. These men were very particular about their harness and often travelled to their favourite saddler in their own time if tack needed to be repaired or altered.

▲ This barn at Tisbury forms part of a large farm-yard complex at Place Farm, formerly a grange of the nunnery of Shaftesbury. This is a remarkable continuity of use from the 14th century, more than 600 years of farming from the same site and mainly in the same buildings. Today the cattle in this photograph of the 1930s have been replaced by a herd of pedigree Holsteins, a variety of Friesian developed in Canada, but the buildings remain largely unaltered. The barn is of the 15th century and is the largest in England but not, at 200 feet, the longest. It originally had stone tiles before being thatched; the thatch seen here was replaced in slightly more ornamental form in 1971.

The Hard Months

THE HARD months, from January to March, could still be severe for both man and beast. Much of the work revolved around the farmyard. Cattle had to be fed, milked and cleaned out. Hay was taken from rick, root crops from clamp and cake from store and all had to be chopped and prepared in the best way to suit different types of stock. Some ploughing might be done on milder days when the great horses would be led out to the fields, steaming gently in the chilly air; otherwise they were chiefly used for jobs of carting – transporting feed, timber, animals and humans. The muck heap in the corner of the yard would grow rapidly, giving a promise of fertility for the coming year.

This was a worrying time for the shepherd, folding the ewes by the means of hurdles on growing root crops, and in heavy falls of snow finding and digging out buried sheep. A shepherd who turned his rams into the flock early might even start lambing before the worst of the weather was gone. All jobs were cold in this weather despite many layers of clothes, stout boots and mittens, hands and feet soon became numb. Working with animals at least provided some warmth from their collective body heat.

During these months the provident farmer overhauled machinery and equipment that would be needed later in the year. Harrows, reapers and binders would be checked and repaired and if badly broken sent to the blacksmith. Hand tools and other implements might receive new wooden handles and cutting edges would be sharpened while leather harness which had taken the strain of the harvest and ploughing was sent to the saddlers for repair. Farms with fences instead of hedges could spend time in repairs, replacing worn out fence lines and gates, dividing some fields with new fences and enlarging others by the removal of old ones. With no leaves on tree or hedge this was a good time for spotting holes in hedgerows and filling them with a bit of barbed wire.

The centre of much activity was the farmhouse kitchen where men looked in for hot drinks and meals throughout the day. In contrast to the cold and wet outside here everything was warm and comfortable and a man could thaw out in front of the welcome heat of the range while clasping a mug of steaming tea, spiced beer, home made wine or cherry brandy. The farmer's wife needed to be a tolerant soul for she had to suffer wet, muddy men in her kitchen throughout the hours of daylight.

Unlike the town dweller the countryman was still in tune with the seasons; his life and work dependent upon the weather. This was a time of year that he did not particularly enjoy and he had to be prepared to cope with blizzards, gales and floods, all of which brought different problems to the farm which had to be solved without our modern means of heavy machinery and helicopters. In outlying areas animals, and occasionally men, were still lost and the happiest time of the day was the early evening when one could relax before a good open fire.

▲ A demonstration in the use of the breast plough for the benefit of the photographer. This plough was the most primitive of all implements of cultivation, being basically a pointed stick which was pushed through the soil to open up a furrow. A later development was a wooden draw hoe which the farmer pulled behind him and which was later harnessed to cattle to become the forerunner of the modern plough. It is possible that this type of plough may have had limited use on smallholdings in the 19th century but it is more likely that this particular implement was made especially for demonstration. A similar tool was used to cut peat in Scotland and Ireland until recent times.

▲ Before the advent of mechanical threshing machines the removal of the grains from the ears of corn was achieved by use of a flail. This back breaking job survived to the end of the 19th century in some places and this picture comes from a generation which would have seen the implement in regular use. When outside winter work became impossible the task of threshing was done in the barn; this was a skilled job as the corn had to be struck just below the ears to avoid damaging the grain as it was shaken loose. After threshing the grain was sieved and then cleaned by being winnowed – thrown up in a draught so that the lighter chaff blew away. Mechanical threshing had appeared during the 1830s and had been the cause of much unrest as men saw their winter work disappearing and the prospect of being laid off for some months looming near. United action by farmers, however, brought about the introduction of the new threshing drum which continued in use until the outbreak of the Second World War. The first combine harvester, enabling threshing to be done as the corn was cut, was not seen in England until 1928 and they were not generally used in Wiltshire until after the end of the Second World War.

◄ An early form of chaff cutter being demonstrated in the barn where it would have been used to provide foodstuffs for animals. It is basically a wooden trough, open at both ends, into which straw or hay is pushed with one hand while the other operates the knife edged lever. This cutter has an added refinement of a treadle, operated by the right foot, which moved a board to hold down the straw while the cut was being made. A further development was to have knives fitted to a wheel, which by a system of toothed rollers enabled the straw to be fed through automatically as the wheel was turned. This was often powered by a steam, gas or petrol engine. Other machines in use during the winter were root shredders, crushing and roller mills and oil cake crushers; all to render food the better suited to the various animals' digestions.

▲ A relic of the harshness of earlier winters was the dovecote which was the prerogative of the lord of the manor. At a time when little fresh meat was available a supply of doves or pigeons was very welcome while at other times the eggs were a useful supplement to those of hens, geese and ducks. The interior of the dovecote at Winterbourne Earls shows the construction of the nesting boxes by the medium of chalk blocks. As times changed and cattle did not have to be slaughtered at the onset of winter, doves were more often kept for ornamental purposes rather than for the pot. By the 20th century if a countryman wanted pigeon pie he shot or trapped wood pigeons, regarded as a great pest. Pigeon pie was not partaken of too frequently, however, as it was often said that after a generous helping you could feel them fluttering in your stomach all night; there is also a country superstition that if you eat a pigeon a day for a week you will be dead.

▲ Carter Will Staples takes a break to pose for the camera at Urchfont in 1932. His costume is fairly traditional with a long waistcoat giving some of the advantages of the modern body warmer. There are signs of wear on the horse collar, normally tailored to the individual requirements of each horse, perhaps indicating either an older horse or a collar reused from an earlier animal. Each horse's harness would hang in the tack room by his nameplate and a great deal of care and attention was paid to cleanliness and condition of this important equipment.

▲ A team of horses on their way to work at West Marden in 1929 use the metalled highway between the farm and the fields. From their heavy collars the shires carry their own nosebags and water containers; groundwater except in the form of dew ponds was a rare occurrence on the chalklands. The leading horse is also carrying the mid-day bait for humans. Working horses were always blinkered to avoid any distractions and to keep them looking ahead when working side by side. One of the skills of the horseman could be seen in the way that the manes, tails and feathers of his charges were cared for and groomed.

▲ An example of ploughing on the chalk is seen at Gore Cross near Market Lavington. What is now a familiar sight of white chalky ploughland, usable only by the intensive application of chemical fertilisers, was at this time a rare picture. Some of Salisbury Plain had been ploughed during the Napoleonic Wars but most of the downland survived until this time. The distant trees are most probably beech, many of which were planted in Wiltshire in the 18th and 19th centuries by landowners anxious to improve the view of not only themselves but also of their neighbours.

▲ After the hard frosts had done their work by cracking the hard clods of earth, the furrow sides were broken up to produce the fine tilth needed for spring sowing. Two implements were used for this, the cultivator for the heavy work and the harrow for producing the tilth. In use here, between Bratton and Imber, on Salisbury Plain are chain harrows; a further development often used for moving soil over grass seed. This harrow was made up by a large number of sharp serrated edged discs which were linked within a chain web.

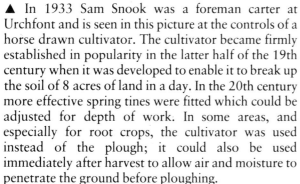

▲ In 1933 Sam Snook was a foreman carter at Urchfont and is seen in this picture at the controls of a horse drawn cultivator. The cultivator became firmly established in popularity in the latter half of the 19th century when it was developed to enable it to break up the soil of 8 acres of land in a day. In the 20th century more effective spring tines were fitted which could be adjusted for depth of work. In some areas, and especially for root crops, the cultivator was used instead of the plough; it could also be used immediately after harvest to allow air and moisture to penetrate the ground before ploughing.

Generally the cultivator was most useful in the small fields of the smaller farms and in the market gardening areas where only a few acres of land needed to be turned over at a time. There was the added advantage that only one horse was needed to draw it, thus cutting down the number of animals on the farm or smallholding.

▲ An important job was returning goodness to the ground in the form of dung which was deposited by cattle in the stockyard during the winter. This superb picture was taken outside the village shop at Keevil in 1934. The horse is being watered from an old galvanised bath while the lad in charge goes to buy his own refreshment at the nearby off licence. The pitchfork stuck in the top of the pile was used for loading as well as for spreading the dung over the fields. In the background the village stores has some signs to indicate its importance as a local institution. It was not only a shop but a centre of village life with its post office, public telephone and parish noticeboard.

The life of most villages still revolved around the farming community. Some farmhouses and their yards were still situated in the middle of the village. This brought the sights, smells and farming patterns to the notice of all inhabitants and children grew up with a good knowledge of the stable, the dairy and the stockyard. With the twice daily walk between pasture and dairy, cattle were as familiar a sight in the street as the farm horse and cart.

42

▲ A tranquil scene after muck spreading near the Lydeway at Etchilhampton. The tethered horse has a blanket over his quarters to prevent him catching a chill after getting hot and sweating from his exertions. Although chemical fertilisers had been used since the 1840s many farmers still relied on mucking their fields. Other natural manures came from the ploughing in of green crops or industrial waste matter such as shoddy from the woollen mills.

Much of the muck spreading was done by pitchfork, often straight off the cart; an operation that required strong arms, shoulders and back to keep a regular swinging motion over a period of several hours. This became very warm exercise and on a frosty morning, steam would be rising from both men and horses and, of course, the muck heap.

Spring and Early Summer

THE LENGTHENING days of late March and early April were as welcome as the cuckoo who arrived during them. Freed from the grip of winter the land was harrowed, rolled and brought into a fit state for spring sowing. Barley and spring wheat would be drilled, to be followed a little later by sowings of cabbages, kale, turnips and mangolds. The supply of stored foodstuffs was coming to an end and a late spring would cause anxious moments and perhaps necessitate the buying in of extra cattle cake or a rick of hay from a better supplied neighbour. An early spring which started the grass into quick growth was a bonus but there was often the feeling that it was too good to last and there was still some bad weather to come.

This was the busiest time of the year for the shepherd who would often live out with his sheep during lambing in March and April. A large flock made for many sleepless nights and the sight of a lantern bobbing around the sheep pens during all the hours of darkness was commonplace. After weaning the new lambs were turned out on to the new grass, often in the water meadows, and given the first bite before the ewes.

Cattle also welcomed the new grass after the winter diet of hay, straw and stored roots, a change often reflected by increased milk yields. As crops germinated and grew, thinning and hoeing were necessary and as the danger of frosts receded field crops of potatoes, peas and beans were planted. The market gardens were busy producing early salad crops and keeping a careful watch on their tender outside vegetables. There were few orchards in Wiltshire but for them this was an anxious time when one freezing night could ruin a season's crop.

On the whole this was a happy burgeoning time. Sap was rising in both plants and animals and everywhere new life was springing forth. The hedgerow elms were wine coloured before bursting into leaf and hiding the untidy nests of rooks. Bare hedges turned to many shades of green and everywhere there was the white blossom of blackthorn and hawthorn. The sturdy shoots of corn pricking the brown ploughland was a promise of later golden wealth while the fecundity of the animal world showed itself in lambs, calves, piglets and chickens to be fattened up for market and table.

The village began to look outside itself again and travel became easier and more pleasant. The effects of spring were noticeable in people too. A younger sprightlier gait replaced the plodding walk and there was a more optimistic outlook on life and its problems. To match the finery of plants and trees new clothes were bought and worn while many a farmer was tempted into buying a new car. Surplus lambs were sent to spring markets while farmers with plenty of good pasture land would buy in cattle to fatten during the summer. As the days became ever longer and the sun grew higher work increased to occupy much of the daylight hours.

▲ This traditional Salisbury Plain picture shows sheep grazing at Stonehenge while in the background a few tourists view the prehistoric monument. Between 1930, when this photograph was taken, and recent years there was a dearth of sheep on the Plain but now they have once again become a familiar sight. Sheep are comparatively undemanding animals and have the ability to feed happily on thin tough pasture and were therefore the ideal grazing animal for this area. The county has its own breed of sheep, the Wiltshire Horn, but by the beginning of the 20th century there were none left in its native domain; there is now one flock in existence. The breed has a poor carcass and instead of wool grows a coat of matted hair which is moulted.

▲ The shepherd's calendar was thus: August – September, the sheep were dipped to kill parasites; October – November, the rams were turned out with the ewes; December – February, the ewes were removed to better pasture in preparation for lambing; March – April, lambing time saw the ewes in shelters often with the shepherd living out with them; May – June, the lambs were turned on to the new grass; July – August, sheep shearing. The shepherd's life was a hard, often lonely one and he not only had to cope with difficult births but the various ailments his sheep were prone to. In this picture a flock is being moved to higher pasture near Woodford in 1939.

Until the 1st World War, sheep were used for distributing their manure over the ground and fertilising the land for crops of wheat and barley which brought money into the farm. These were known as arable, or hurdle, sheep and were almost always the breed called Hampshire Downs. This system had required a great deal of labour and when labour and feeding stuffs became scarce and the price of lambs and wool dropped, the Hampshire Downs were gradually killed off and not replaced. As they disappeared, their place was taken by Cheviots and Blackfaces which, being grass sheep, required less labour and were able to graze the downs which rapidly became enclosed with wire fences.

◄ Lambing was the busiest time of the year for the shepherd. The pregnant ewes were penned in one small area and shelters constructed of hurdles to provide cover for the ewes when giving birth. Smaller pens were used for ewes with lambs so that a careful watch could be kept on their progress. Very often the shepherd lived on the downs with his sheep, eating and sleeping in a small wooden hut. Food was still often carried up into the hills by his wife or children and the shepherd lived by himself for 6 to 8 weeks although sometimes it was possible to fold sheep near to the shepherd's cottage so that he might get home occasionally.

◄ This portrait of a shepherd near Bratton in 1912 shows an independent weather beaten man with his smock, crook and short-stemmed pipe. At this time shepherds were quite autocratic and many farms revolved around the needs of the sheep with the shepherd's word as law. Apart from lambing and a few other busy times there was much opportunity for carving crooks and contemplation. In *Farmer's Glory,* published in 1932, A.G. Street tells a nice story of a newcomer to farming who discovered his shepherd dozing under a bush on the downs. On being asked what he was doing he replied, 'lookin' atter your sheep' and on being further pressed stated that he was studying his master's interests. A.G. Street estimated that apart from his busy times a shepherd could reckon on finishing his laborious work by dinner time; after that he quite properly studied his master's sheep.

▲ While the farm often seemed to be run for the sheep the cattle men suspected that it was largely due to the money received for milk that the farm remained financially sound. In the 1920s the open air system of dairying became established. With this cattle were milked twice a day in the field by means of a mobile milking parlour. This included stalls for 6 cows and a power plant for the milking machine and electric lighting. By these methods milking could be done by 2 men and the cows folded over the fields enriching the land as they fed. In a time of agricultural depression the amount of labour and money saved by these means was often the difference between solvency and bankruptcy. The heifers in the field near Urchfont, however, have not yet reached the stage of their introduction to the milking machine.

The mobile milking parlour had been invented by Mr. Hosier, a farmer of Wexcombe, near Marlborough, and was widely used in the county of its inventor. The system meant that the farmer could concentrate solely on milk production and not have to keep man and machines to tend arable land. This often led to better milk yields with the cows being in the fresh air all the time, keeping cleaner, and in consequence happier, while the farmer, specialising in his cattle, was able to learn more about them and improve his stock. Cows were milked at 4.30 a.m. and 2.30 p.m.; between these times, the milking parlour was moved to fresh ground, while in winter, hay was carried to the cattle for morning and evening feeds.

▲ This splendid picture from Easterton shows a carter and his horse. It was noticeable with older countrymen that however hot it became they rarely removed their waistcoat, or 'weskit' as they would have said, and often wore a vest as well to 'soak up the sweat'. At one time these horses' tails were docked, the lower 6 joints amputated with a special docking iron, to prevent the long point of the tail being injured when the horse was harnessed to the cart. This operation is now illegal and fortunately all horses are able to keep their fine tails.

▲ On a mixed farm the hens were normally the prerequisites of the farmer's wife and a large flock was often held to be a sign of petticoat government. At Manor Farm, near Lydeway, between Etchilhampton and Wedhampton, in 1929, a small flock of hens and turkeys are being fed. Small flocks of fowls could be kept in the farmyard by day, where they cleared up spilt grain, waste and insects, and were locked in the hen house at night to protect them from foxes. Larger flocks were kept in runs, well fenced orchards or paddocks; these would need supplementary feeding although they still found a lot of food for themselves, including such pests as wire worms. The large flocks were run commercially but the smaller ones of hens, ducks, geese and turkeys would provide eggs and birds for the kitchen table with the profits of any surplus going to the lady of the house.

49

◀ If the income from fowls was taken by the farmer's wife that from pigs, on many farms, was the prerequisite of the son. Mr. E. Plank feeds his Large Whites in 1929 at Wedhampton, in a farmyard also inhabited by hens and ducks. The pig is a most economical animal, converting by-products from other farming operations into good solid flesh, and was to be found on most dairy farms in weatherproof styes which opened out into small yards. In better weather pigs could be allowed to forage for themselves and a group would act as very efficient cultivators if old pasture land needed to be broken up. If, however, they were kept on good pasture a ring through the nose was necessary to prevent them rootling up the ground in search of insects and roots.

▲ Early one morning in 1927, 5 horse teams set off to work from Horton crossing the canal bridge by a dusty, chalky road. This picture emphasises the large number of horses kept on the farm at this period, despite the fact that by 1918 there were already 140 different makes of tractor on the market. The Great War had changed the farmer's attitude to tractors when it became obvious that if England was to be self sufficient in food more power was needed than could be provided by the horse. Even so, many farmers preferred to use teams of horses up to and through the Second World War.

▲ This carter with his team of horses is pictured at Easton Piercy, near Coate, in 1928. In the background is the light wain from which the animals have been unhitched. A wide variety of carts and wagons were used for different jobs and each county had its own distinctive type, best suited to the local ground conditions. The heavy farm wagon became popular in the 19th century, when larger and stronger horses were bred, and it was still in use after the Second World War. The wagon was a masterpiece of the arts of the carpenter and wheelwright and one man might make 7 or 8 of these in a year.

▲ A team of 3 horses pull this chain harrow near Bishops Cannings in 1928. The harrow is probably being used to remove dead grass from established grassland and so encourage fresh growth. The horse on the right has an engraved piece of brass or leather on its head, a feature that was becoming unusual at this period when most of the old horse brasses were lying neglected in the tack room or had been rescued and carefully restored for house decorations by the newcomers to rural life.

51

▲ The agricultural depression of the 1930s led to many farms being neglected, run down or abandoned. This was a busy time for auctioneers as some farmers were unable to pay their debts and had to watch while the whole of the 'live and dead' farming stock, which they had so carefully built up, came under the hammer before a cheery crowd and to the accompaniment of much badinage. This picture shows a rather neglected corner of Hill Farm, Urchfont, in 1937 with derelict buildings and rampant nettles, or 'ettles' as they are more frequently called in Wiltshire. When the outbreak of war seemed inevitable land prices rose as many businessmen realised that whatever happened to stocks, shares and commodities the farmlands of England would not disappear overnight and would provide a good investment for the war years.

Haysel and Harvest

THERE are of course many harvests but the most notable two are those of hay and corn. First comes haysel with its pictures of sun burned men, women, and often children who had missed school to help get the hay in. After mowing, the hay was tossed and turned, normally by machine until it was dry enough to be gathered. Then came the well-remembered scenes of pitching the hay on to the top of wagons while the great horses stood patiently between the shafts. A long haul to the rickyard followed where the hay was made into ricks and thatched with straw. Most Wiltshire people over the age of 40 can remember helping with, or watching this activity and pictures of it release a flood of memories. It was always a race against the weather and constant showers could ruin the hay and leave a farm short of winter feed or later give rise to a hot rick and a fire in the yard.

Other, and more minor harvests, were apples, pears and soft fruits while vegetables included peas, beans and potatoes. Later on, other root crops such as turnips, swedes and mangolds were lifted and stored in barn and clamp. Throughout this season both men and horses worked long hours whenever the sun shone, for every hour was precious and there was always the thought that some days would be wasted because of wet weather.

On sheep farms this was the time of shearing when gangs of shearers travelled from farm to farm during July and August to relieve the sheep of their heavy hot fleeces. Smaller farms might well do their own shearing but the larger flocks needed the skill and expertise of the professional shearer. With the powered clippers which were being introduced each sheep would take between two and four minutes to shear but with older equipment a longer time was required.

The last harvest was corn; wheat, barley and oats, the rolling golden acres were gradually reaped by the slow moving machines which tossed out the bound sheaves to be stacked into stooks. These were later collected and taken to the farmyard to be threshed out. The grain was then stored in the granary and the straw compacted for use during the winter months. One well known voice of those days is now silent, that summer visitor the corncrake no longer breeds in southern England and his harsh grating call no longer accompanies the months before harvest. Something else now missing is the shooting of rabbits as they bolted from the last remaining corn, a practice not only changed by machinery but also by myxomatosis.

Many customs, predating the Christian harvest home, survive in rural counties. These vary from area to area but many involve a corn dolly woven from the last sheaf. It was normally proper to have a harvest supper, paid for by the farmer, with plenty to eat and drink. Thanks to the seasons which had brought in turn, clay breaking frosts, gentle rains, warmth and finally dry weather, could be given with proper respect. Later the older men would allow themselves to be persuaded to sing the mystical, obscure or roistering songs that were at the end of a long oral tradition. Tomorrow would bring ploughing, for the seasons are always there to be obeyed and when the full circle has turned one must start again, but first that night would see a good pagan celebration.

◄ Sheep shearing took place in July and August and in the case of larger flocks was often undertaken by contract gangs. At Hill Farm, Great Cheverell, Messers Bell and Webb are tackling the long and arduous task which required a great deal of skill and the ability to work fast. Powered shearing cutters are in use which enabled the shearers to concentrate on holding the sheep steady and guiding the cutters over its body. Before the introduction of these powered cutters the shearer also had to perform the clipping action with one hand; even so an expert could shear up to 50 sheep in a day. About a week before shearing the sheep were normally washed, to remove dirt from the fleece, in specially constructed washing pools early in the morning so that the sun could dry out the fleece during the day.

▲ Wheat grows best on heavy soil with a fair amount of clay in its make up. During the hard times of the 1920s and 30s large scale cereal farming became one of the few economic propositions in the county. Then labour could be drastically reduced and superphosphates used to encourage continuous corn growing. Occasionally the bare land was allowed to lie fallow for a year to clean it. This was one of the developments which was to mark the breakaway from labour intensive farming into one where a large capital investment was needed for machinery. The large wheatfields seen from Redhorn Hill have already been cut.

◄ It is certain that if town dwellers of today were asked for their impressions of farming life in the past, 9 out of 10 would first mention haymaking. It has created a lasting feeling of affection — many of us having been allowed to help, or more probably hinder, in our young days. In retrospect the sun never seemed to cease shining, rain was unheard of at haysel and the grass dried into sweet smelling hay which never went sour or caused a hot rick. In practice of course there were as many wet days as there are now and the horse drawn tedder, used to turn the drying hay, would rarely have seen continuous action. The horse drawn rake was used to deposit the dry hay into straight neat rows to facilitate picking up. The camera has caught 2 of these teams having their mid day bait at the foot of Silbury Hill.

◄ At Wedhampton in 1930 the dried piles of hay are being pitchforked on to a Wiltshire wagon. Normally one or two men pitched from the ground while one man on top ensured an even distribution. On arrival in the farmyard the hay was compressed into bales and made into ricks. On less modern farms a baler may not have been used and the hay pitched directly from wagon to rick. Rick making was a skilled job and at the end of the day the expertise of thatching was also required to provide a waterproof top.

▲ At haymaking time everyone lent a hand, men, women and children would be involved, although not in such arduous work as before mechanisation. Then the drying hay was turned by women, throwing it into the air to open it up to the sun. In the 1920s and 30s women and children were most likely to be used for light work and providing refreshment while older boys tried their hand at pitching. In this refreshment break near All Cannings jars of cider and beer and bottles of cold tea are well in evidence. When not in use the safest place for a pitchfork was stuck upright in the ground or hay where its sharp tines could not injure anyone.

▲ During haymaking a large number of wagons were needed to transport the hay from the fields to the rickyard. With the ever present threat of the weather breaking it was important that men should not be standing idle in either place so there must always be empty wagons to load and full ones to unload. By the amount of dung in the road it would seem that this route at Foxley Corner, Urchfont was well used by several teams gathering the hay while the sun shone. On the return journey the empty wagon provided an exciting ride for small children who might not get many other opportunities to travel other than on their own two feet.

◄ After the work of the day men and horses were glad to make their way home to the farmyard. Working throughout the day in the hayfields was strength sapping, throat parching work. Dust and pollen abounded and eyes, nose and throat would all suffer. At Horton in 1928 these 3 teams take an old sunken road which gives a few welcome patches of shade.

▲ An important development in the 19th century had been the reaper which ended the labourer's day long toil over scythe or sickle, although the sheaves still had to be gathered, tied and stooked by hand. Later in the century a further advance came from America with the introduction of the first binder which cut the corn and carried it on a canvas belt to the binder where it was pressed into a sheaf, tied and thrown out. This became the chief implement of the corn harvest until the widespread use of combines in the 1950s. In 1927 this binder, with its 3 horse team was used near Monument Hill at Etchilhampton.

▲ A picture especially posed for the benefit of the photographer in 1938 by 2 ladies of Great Cheverell, wearing the styles of 50 years before. This does, however, serve to illustrate the hard work of harvest before the introduction of the binder. After reaping, whether by scythe or mechanical means, the corn had to be tied up in sheaves. In the early days teams of between 7 and 10 people composed of reapers, gatherers and men to tie and stook would cut from 2 to 3 acres a day. The mechanical reaper deposited the corn in rows, or regular bunches, on the ground from where it was gathered, tied and stooked by both men and women.

◀ James Drew of Etchilhampton gazes over a large expanse of corn stooks in 1927. His leather gaiters were favoured by the older men, especially at harvest time when they protected the lower leg from the sharp stubble. If one is allowed to put thoughts into his head we can suppose that he is probably reflecting on the ease of the modern harvest compared with the dusty, sticky days of his youth when although the scythe would cut so sweetly in the early morning dew, as the sun rose higher each stroke became more and more arduous. Only one year after this picture was taken the first combine harvester appeared in Britain from America.

◀ In the ominous months before the outbreak of the Second World War farming life still followed its normal pattern although most countrymen knew that hostilities were inevitable. When this photograph was taken at Hill Farm, Great Cheverell, in 1939 though there could have been no thought that the declaration of war by Great Britain on September 3rd was to have such a dramatic effect on all farming processes. The corn was still carried by horse-drawn wagon from field to farmyard for the threshing; it had always been thus, surely it would always be so. Lowland Wiltshire was still basically a patchwork pattern of small fields with good hedgerow timber not yet sacrificed to the needs of big and expensive machinery.

◀ A lasting impression of harvest was the beer or cider that slaked hot and dusty throats. A few farms still made their own, a more potent brew than that of the commercial manufacturers, which created vivid impressions in both mind and body, best recorded by Laurie Lee in a Cotswold village not many miles from the Wiltshire border. The effect of some other ciders was to give the brain a bright and clear perception of all things whilst taking away the means of locomotion from a man, thus enabling him to sing and discourse freely while having to remain firmly fixed in one spot. No such occurrences are commemorated by this picture which has been set up in 19th century dress for the camera, but the costeril, or plough bottle, is one of many that were taken to the edge of the field for the refreshment of thirsty workers during the day.

61

▲ One of the disappearing features of the countryside is the pond – ponds that could be counted on to provide children with tadpoles or newts are long gone – filled in for the sake of better drainage by farmers who can now provide their cattle with water piped to the field. But in the 1920s and 30s the pond was an important part of the farming economy and summer scenes that stay in the memory must include one of cows, tails swishing at the flies, standing up to their hocks in the pond beneath the sun sheltering trees. This pond, near Urchfont, is on the greensand and gault and has probably only needed a little help from man to form. On the porous chalk, however, complex man-made ponds were created to provide water for animals in upland areas. These were the dew ponds and their construction was a specialised skill. Basically, puddled clay formed a lining through which water could not escape to the chalk, but the secret lay in siting the pond so that it was filled from a large catchment area which would always provide more water from normal rainfall than was lost by evaporation.

Rural Crafts

Most countrymen were craftsmen in a way that is becoming increasingly rare today. A farmer, or farm labourer might have to turn his hand to any job: ploughing, harrowing, rolling, sowing, hoeing, reaping, binding, threshing, storing and muck spreading. He had to deal with animals from birth onwards, feeding them and looking after them in pregnancy and sickness. On any day jobs such as repairing machinery or gates, hedging, ditching, walling, fencing or tree felling might need to be done. He would even repair the tractor, though openly despising it and preferring his horses who did not break down. He would often know the best places for catching fish, where the rabbit runs were and how to take a sleeping pheasant from a low branch. At home perhaps he was a proud gardener who carried off prizes for marrows or onions at the village flower show. Most countrymen would have a go at any task and make a reasonble job of it, though they normally only grudgingly admitted that they had made 'a rough old bodge of it'.

The craftsmen we are looking at here are those who specialised in work which their neighbours were glad to pay for. On the outliers of the Cotswolds that enter Wiltshire many farmworkers could make or repair a bit of dry stone walling but the great ribbons of stone flowing over the hills were created by the wallers. Men who had learned their trade as young boys helping their fathers by filling in the centre of the wall with clean rubble. Men who could look at pieces of stone and see their relationship with one another and how each would fit into a course when held in roughened, calloused hands which, with a bent back, was the hallmark of a dry stone waller. In lowland areas where stone was not easily available the skill of laying a hedge had developed to create a barrier through which even the most determined of animals could not penetrate.

Stone was quarried in Wiltshire from the Corsham, Box and Bradford on Avon area in the west and the Nadder valley at Chilmark in the south. Quarrying was a skilled occupation where an extensive knowledge of stone and its weathering was required. Masons to work the stone were scattered throughout the county and some villages had a monumental stone mason who could produce carved stone for any purpose and not only as memorials for the dead.

The skills of workers in stone, as well as those in wood and metal, were needed by the miller. The dressing of the grinding stones was a very technical job and although some millers could do this themselves many used the services of the millwright. At this period there were still some 35 water powered mills in

Wiltshire and the great wooden wheels and the machinery to transfer power from the vertical to horizontal plane required the craft of the carpenter. Several mills were situated in towns but many, mainly those powered by water, worked in the villages where the miller not only ground corn but often baked bread and, even in the 20th century, still cooked joints, pies and cakes for villagers who had no oven in their own home.

Working with timber tended to produce easy going, amiable people and there were many such workers in this period. Men who could look at a growing tree, assess its cubic content and, from its shape and situation, judge the quantity of timber within. Sawyers who would cut a tree into planks to obtain the best effects of strength of the grain and then spend up to 10 years drying and seasoning it. Country carpenters and joiners not only made floors, windows and roofs for new houses but often some of the items needed to furnish them. The craft of wagon building was coming to an end as the great wains, which lasted for so many years before wearing out, were outmoded by the increasing use of the internal combustion engine. The wagons were masterpieces of ingenuity and at their best displayed the finest examples of craftsmanship. They were built by carpenters and wheelwrights, often the 2 trades being combined in one man, and the skills were handed down from father to son. The blacksmith played his part when the wheels had to be shod with iron and the whole was painted in gay colours, by a man who probably ground and mixed his own paints, which remained bright and fresh for decades afterwards.

Of the coppice crafts only hurdle and wattle making survived to any extent in the county at this period. Men, often working alone in woodland, would produce hurdles for sheep pens and wattles for fencing. Apart from a few families of gypsies, basket making was concentrated in the towns and the frails, tool baskets, hampers, trugs and shopping baskets would be bought in the local market town. Today it is difficult to realise how many different types of baskets were used in the country for industry, trade, farm and household before the days of plentiful cardboard and modern packaging.

Most villages still possessed a smith or farrier who could fettle up many of the metal objects that were needed by the countryman. At this time, rather than by a spreading chestnut tree, the smithy was normally distinguished by a heap of old iron outside but the smith was as skilled a craftsman as ever and still held steady the hooves of the mighty shires. Although there were plenty of hunters there were less other riding horses than today but the work of the farrier was maintained to some extent by the racing stables. These provided another facet of craftsmanship in the training of young horses to be champion flat racers and steeplechasers. The well drained springy turf of the downs is well suited to race horse training and many famous names have been associated with such places as Beckhampton, Manton and Marlborough.

Other needs of horses were catered for by the saddlers and harness makers whose workshops greatly attracted the countryman who often had leather harness or articles such as school satchels that needed repair. Although machines were being used increasingly for stitching many men still rightly maintained that hand stitching was far stronger and for a good long lasting job did not use their machines. Glovemaking was an industry common in Wiltshire but by this time most of the work was done in the factory rather than in people's homes. The bootmaker however, was still able to earn a living in several villages although the work was poorly paid and no young men would take up the trade. Before the universal use of rubber boots on the farm the countryman liked a good pair of locally made leather boots and often spent much of his harvest pay on such a pair. To be well shod was essential and far more important than being fashionably dressed and if country made boots did not look very grand at least their wearer's feet were dry and comfortable and probably ached less than those of his successor wearing modern footwear. The bootmaker tailored each pair to the individual and also made a repair that would outlast any pair of mass produced boots or shoes.

Unfortunately the day of the country craftsman was drawing to a close. People preferred cheap mass-produced goods to long lasting quality. A revival had occurred in the 19th century led by men appalled at the shoddiness of Victorian goods but now increased demands were only able to be met by the factory, and young men no longer wished to spend years in low paid apprenticeships when they could earn good money by performing simpler tasks at conveyor belts. In recent years the craftsman in stone, wood, metal and leather is again appreciated and another resurgence is on its way.

Timber was the most valuable material in the countryside, being used by carpenters, wheelwrights, joiners, hurdle makers, basket makers and thatchers. Several villages possessed saw mills, that at Urchfont being run by Maurice Goodman, catering for the needs of the locality and often the nearby town. The sawyers would normally buy the growing trees whose quality they could assess before the timber was felled and removed to the mill. Wood was well seasoned and an elm tree could lie for a year where it was felled before being lifted and sawn into planks. The timber was then stacked in an open sided shelter, like that behind Mr. Goodman, for a further 3 to 10 years. Carpenters did not wish to use any but properly seasoned wood.

▲ The blacksmith was one of the best known people in the village; in 1935 there were still more than 170 smiths and farriers in Wiltshire. The smith could turn his hand to most tasks involving metal; making and mending farm machinery, making edged tools, garden implements, gates and wall plates as well as shoeing horses. With the spread of motor transport he was often called in to straighten out parts of motor cars after collisions and so he kept pace with modern demands. This building which had been used as a smithy at Steeple Langford, with the anvil outside, was formerly a dove cote.

▲ Before the days of easily available mass produced china and cheap plastics the breaking of a piece of china was not necessarily also the time to dispose of it. Several of the pieces had probably been handed down through the family and had acquired the status of heirlooms. So one waited for the regular visit of the china riveter, seen here in 1925, who, with his small hand machine, would repair the plate, bowl or cup. He was one of a disappearing army of itinerant workers who were able to make a living repairing things that we now throw away. Best known of these was the tinker who would patch up many a pot, pan or kettle thus saving the owner a trip to town to buy a new one.

67

▲ In sheep country the art of hurdle making was still of great importance. At lambing time large quantities of hurdles were needed to pen both expectant ewes and newly born lambs while in wintertime they were needed to fold the sheep on growing root crops. The Marlborough Downs were good sheep country and this hurdle maker, seen at Ramsbury in 1935, would have been kept busily employed. It was a solitary occupation for a man who owned or leased a small wood and who needed to understand when and how to best cut and use the coppice wood. Poles were cut in the autumn to the various lengths required and then split with a slim bladed, long headed axe. Often the hurdle maker would undertake all his work in the wood, rarely seeing anyone during his working day.

◀ Harry Fuller was a saddler and harness maker at Urchfont when he was photographed in 1931. Great reliance was placed on the harness maker as if his work was faulty dangerous accidents could ensue for carters and horsemen. Ropemaking was not generally practised in the county at this time, most farmers buying rope and twine manufactured by large firms or imported from abroad. Mr Fuller still seems to have operated a rope walk or he may have brought out his old equipment to show the cameraman how the fibres were twisted into rope.

▲ A joyous sight in the country is a well laid, stockproof hedge but now unfortunately Wiltshire has only a few miles of properly laid hedgerows. The hedger and ditcher was a familiar sight, cutting and laying the new growth then clearing the adjacent ditch to let the winter rains drain freely from the land. Autumn and early winter would be marked by damp piles of dark alluvium and the pleasant tang of woodsmoke rising from bonfires of the useless trimmings. Larger sticks would have been carefully preserved for bean poles or pea sticking for the cottage garden.

▲ Thatching is a craft for which there has been greater demand in recent years than for some decades with more and more people buying and restoring country cottages. In the 1930s it was still the original villagers who employed the thatcher either to patch, put in a new ridge or completely reroof a house. Wheat straw was normally used although the more expensive Norfolk reed was better; it was said that this would last a lifetime. Herbert Daniel Giddings, thatcher of Chirton, is seen in 1933 at work holding the hazel sways that were used to fix the bunches of straw. The hazel would often be bought from the hurdle maker thus saving the thatcher the time taken in finding and cutting it.

▲ In 1933 these new houses at Cuckoo Corner, Urchfont, were thatched despite almost universal use of tile or slate for modern buildings at this period. In the 1930s there were 21 thatchers working in the county and seeing a modern house roofed in the traditional way must have given them a great feeling of pride. In the picture the straw is as yet untrimmed while a pile of hazel lies on the ground ready to be cut into spars and sways. The thatcher's bicycle is propped up at the rear of the building. Today this pair of houses are still nicely thatched.

▲ The long job nears completion at Horton. The nature of straw or reed allowed valleys, dormers and gables to be easily incorporated in a thatched roof giving an overall soft appearance with no harsh lines or angles. In this roof hazel spars have been used to give a decorative effect at the eaves. The thatch pictured here in the 1930s was only renewed 2 or 3 years ago. Other changes have been the painting of the brick infill white and the removal of the water pump. The wheat straw used in thatching was especially grown and cut as modern binders and threshing machines would ruin it for this purpose.

The Countryman's Home

Houses constructed from locally available building materials create an homogenous landscape where nothing appears alien or out of place. A fine stone town such as Bradford on Avon is rooted in the limestone of its bedrock, a building of brick or cob would look totally out of keeping. Put this town on Salisbury Plain though and it would lose much of its appeal, the fine stone architecture would be wrong in an area where small cottages nestle into narrow valleys and folds of the hills to become one with the natural landscape.

A wide variety of building materials were used throughout Wiltshire and certain broad generalisations can be made, although there are always many exceptions to the rule. In the east and south, the Marlborough Downs and Salisbury Plain, the buildings are mainly constructed of brick, brick with flint, or timber and brick, but buildings of stone and cob are also in evidence. To the north and west stone and timber are common and from the 19th century onwards the demand for housing caused most construction to be of brick, although this is most noticeable in the towns.

Despite the varied materials of the walls it tends to be the roof that provides the greatest visual impact of buildings in the countryside. Wiltshire has 3 roofing materials; thatch in the south and east, clay pantiles in the north west and stone slates on the fringes of Cotswold. In many places these traditional forms have been superseded by Welsh slates and modern tiles.

Until the 20th century most rural homes had provided shelter for many successive generations. The majority of people rented their house or lived in a cottage tied to a farm or estate. This provided little security for the farmworker but on the other hand it did enable him to move from job to job and place to place more freely than if he owned his own home. For many people home ownership was financially impossible and unless property was inherited most people continued to pay rent out of their limited income.

The vernacular buildings fell into 2 noticeable categories, the 'big' houses and rectories, and the cottages and small houses of the labourer and craftsmen. The larger houses were either mellow stone or timber framed buildings several centuries old, or else more recent gracious stone and brick homes of the 18th and 19th centuries. It was these latter that often used imported building materials and provided the earliest signs of change to methods of local construction that had lasted several centuries. Almost without exception the builders of all these houses consciously or, more often than not in earlier centuries, unconsciously added to the beauty of the landscape.

Some of the earlier manors and farmhouses suffered a decline in fortune which lasted into the early 20th century. When a landowner or big farmer built a new house his old residence often passed to a yeoman or small farmer. As they and their family prospered and moved on to more modern accommodation the house was often divided to provide homes for farm labourers and by 1900 many former manor houses were giving shelter to up to half a dozen families. This trend has now reversed as people can afford larger houses for smaller families.

Although conditions improved somewhat from the 19th century many aspects of rural accommodation were still primitive. Gas and electricity were unknown in many homes and piped water had not reached some rural areas. Lighting was by means of oil lamps while cooking was often on a coal or wood burning range which, with open fires, provided heat during the winter. Water from the well or pump sometimes in a outhouse, more often in the garden, and an earth closet provided the other services that are taken for granted today. Bringing in water, collecting and cutting fire wood and logs, and digging a new hole when the earth closet needed moving, all took time. The first daily task for many children was pumping or drawing water and all the family brought back pieces of wood from a walk.

Shorter working hours provided better opportunities for a labourer to cultivate his vegetable patch and many cottages could now boast a well tended plot providing food for the kitchen, as well as the traditional flower garden of lupins, cornflowers, columbines and sunflowers. Often a pig sty and hen run completed the picture thus providing a degree of self sufficiency in several basic foodstuffs. Inside the cottage there was often some very good pieces of furniture handed down through the family and some locally made items of varying quality. Very frequently, however, furniture and other possessions were fairly simple and were purchased in the market and shops of a nearby town, or secondhand at auction.

Somewhere between the two main categories of dwellings in this period were the farmhouses. In the dairying areas the farms were small and the farmhouse was sometimes little bigger than the labourer's cottage. Most farmhouses, however, were of reasonable size and many had been in the same family for generations. Here, 'where all's accustomed ceremonious' the furniture was normally good solid oak which had been handed down from generation to generation and the big kitchens were well equipped with shining pots, pans and coppers. Often sides of bacon hung in the roof while fruits, vegetables and pickles were bottled each in their season.

The greatest change in the life of the countryman was his increased awareness of the larger world outside of his immediate boundaries. Unlike his forbears he could read and write and had access to a daily newspaper. Even if the home did not possess a radio, run off rechargeable accumulator batteries, the news and opinions were relayed at the village shop or pub. Day trips to the seaside, Bristol, Southampton or London produced a broader outlook while the survivors of the Great War experienced places that had previously only been names in a school atlas. This awareness provoked a desire for more possessions and a better standard of living.

The following photographs show a little of the variety of the countryman's home. The materials vary from area to area while the period of construction may be from any one of seven centuries. One labourer might live in a thatched medieval manor while his fellow worker lived in a 1920s farm cottage with all amenities; a farmer in a 14th century monastic grange while his friend in the next village resided in a Georgian mansion. No matter what the building it was as much a part of the local landscape as the beech clump on the hill, the 200 year old oak or even the downs themselves.

▲ Lacock is one of the best villages in the county with a compact square of streets mainly composed of medieval buildings. Much of the village, with Lacock Abbey, was given to the National Trust by Matilda Talbot, a descendant of Sir William Sharington who had bought and converted the Abbey at the Dissolution of the Monasteries. There is still a fine sense of Tudor times, here illustrated by Porch House at the end of the High Street, and the village was as much a tourist attraction between the wars as it is now. Lacock is a good example of a community where most of the property was owned by one family who managed to keep the village intact while ensuring that it did not become fossilized in the past.

◄ The village shop often sold everything from cheese to corsets and moth balls to mousetraps. With people taking trips into town only infrequently the shopkeeper was called upon to provide the many varied items that the countryman needed. In 1930 the shop at Bromham was housed in a fine timber-framed jettied building which is now an antique shop. Beyond the shop is the stone built inn, the Greyhound, which with the nearby church of St. Nicholas would act as the focal points of village life.

◄ Many farm labourers lived in tied cottages and keeping a roof over their heads was dependent upon them retaining their jobs. In 1928 a labourer from Manor Farm at Stert, near Devizes, returns home to his thatched timber-framed cottage where he is greeted by his children at the farm gate. This cottage was part of the farm complex situated on the edge of the farmyard with a thatched barn to the rear. Today it is barely recognisable; the farther end has been extended by one bay and the chimney stack reduced while the friendly compatible thatch has been replaced by tiles.

◄ A superb thatched early timber-framed house at Oare, the Old Oxyard, is secluded from the main road by the thatched stalls, seen in the foreground, that were probably built for housing cattle. In the 1930s this was the residence of a justice of the peace. All villages possessed some fine houses in which local gentry and successful businessmen lived, bringing a more cosmopolitan air to the place and providing glimpses of more exotic worlds to the other villagers. Oare itself had several big houses, including Oare House, at this time the home of Sir Geoffrey Fry, later to become the residence of Sir Anthony Eden. Today the Oxyard is unchanged, it has been rethatched but the only alteration seems to be the addition of 2 straw pigeons over the doorway.

▲ Redundant rectories and vicarages seem to be recent phenomena yet this photograph of 1930 shows one such, the Old Rectory at Rollestone, Shrewton. Shrewton is an interesting village consisting of 5 former parishes; Maddington, Orcheston St. Mary, Orcheston St. George, Rollestone and Shrewton. The first 4 remain only as parish fields, churches and the names of farms and manors. Rollestone possesses the oldest church, a small flint one dating back to the 13th century, which with this former rectory and Rollestone Manor, now a large farm, make an attractive group. In 1930 apart from these the settlement consisted of 4 or 5 scattered old thatched houses; today it has grown considerably but the substantial rectory is largely unchanged although now it is surrounded by fine landscaped gardens.

▲ Besides being a home for the landlord and his family the village pub provided a home from home for many of its regulars. The pub was not merely a place for drinking; it was a social club and community centre, a place where a man could take his problems, tell stories, exchange gossip and opinions and enjoy a good sing song. Darts, dominoes, cards and skittles would be played while the cricket and football teams would take a drink after their game. They and many other teams and groups would also hold their meetings in the back room. In the 1930s a small social revolution occurred which had happened much earlier in the towns. The countrywomen started to go to the pub with their menfolk and so this aspect of village life was broadened and improved; no longer need women sit at home wondering if their men would come back sober or not. Thus the pub was second only to the church in the established life of the village dispensing not only beer and spirits but also warmth, laughter and companionship. Very often the bar would serve several small rooms where grave old men could sit in quiet conversation or play crib surreptitiously for money. Beer from a local brewery would be tapped 24 hours before use and served from wooden barrels behind the bar. Wadworths Brewery at Devizes supplied the thatched Lamb Inn at Rowde which was unfortunately destroyed by fire in 1938.

▲ A tranquil corner of an English village. Thatched barns and walls encompass the farmyard which crowds around the long farmhouse. The church of St. Giles keeps watch over the 152 souls of the parish while those of a non-conformist persuasion could attend the Baptist chapel that had been built in 1839. All villages change but this one more than most; for this is Imber in the years before the Army evacuated the village in 1943 as a 'temporary measure' to provide a further training ground on the Plain. Now Imber has been wiped out and the only reasonably intact building remaining is the church. Even before the Second World War living here must have been a little unnerving as the War Department had gradually acquired all the surrounding land and life was punctuated by soldiers, tanks and crumps from the firing ranges.

▲ A pleasant example of diaper work at Barford St. Martin is, in 1930, attached to a building faced with lath and plaster. This latter building typifies the decline of some villages at this period when many farms were running at a loss thus depriving a village of its chief source of wealth. For when times are hard for farmers less hands are employed and tradesmen take less money and suffer more bad debts. Some people would have been forced to quit their village and look for work in the towns, though in this they would often be unlucky as by now the towns had many hundreds of their own unemployed. The building on the left of this picture has now been refaced in stone while the other part is greatly altered and the whole of the thatched roof replaced with flat tiles.

▲ The times when the life of the village was centred upon the manor house had gone but the local squire still exercised some influence. Often he was the largest local employer and occasionally he would take the welfare of the whole village on his shoulders, although this latter might not always be to the ultimate benefit of the community. The manor house conjures up pictures of garden parties, peach trees cosseted by gardeners, croquet, tennis and the sadly missed country house cricket. This cricket was bowled out by the advent of the Second World War. Until then the head gardener would spend long hours preparing the wicket and during the season the house party would play local village sides and touring teams such as the Free Forester or elevens made up from the artistic and literary communities. This particular house was at Imber and remarkably is still partially in existence.

▲ A timber-framed building here provides a home for 2 families whereas originally this was a single farmhouse. The thatch is in good condition and with brick nogging between the timbers the occupants should have been fairly snug. The small windows would have created a need for longer hours of artificial light than might have been economically possible with the number of candle or oil lamps that would be needed. Large families could be brought up in these cottages and although toys might be scarce there would be a large garden and all the nearby fields, woods and streams to be explored and, farmers permitting, used for games. A child's life would rarely have been dull for although there might be a few neighbours the busy life of the farmyard and the ever changing natural world would provide not only pleasure but a more enjoyable education than could be obtained from schoolbooks.

▲ A very solid and substantial stone and timber framed house in the Kennet valley. The right hand section seems to be the earliest part with an interesting gable and framing infilled with brick. The stone section was probably added as the family grew or a son married and needed space for his own family. This piecemeal building and extending has made for the attractive old houses and cottages to be seen in every village. An interesting feature here is the dry walling of good sized stones. These come from the split remains of local sarsen stones which are to be found all around the source of the Kennet and which in an earlier age were used to create Avebury. Their use in this wall gives the finishing touch to the value of using local materials. These include the local stone of the cottage, timber from Savernake Forest, clay brick from Pewsey Vale and thatching straw from the nearby fields.

▲ A good example of the changing occupancy of a home is seen in the Old Manor House at Bromham. Originally a timber framed manor with its own lands and farms, it became old fashioned in the late 17th or 18th centuries when the owners would have built a modern residence. It doubtless passed to a farmer wealthy enough to maintain it but not rich enough, or unduly concerned with fashion, to live in a new property. We can conjecture that the building had several farmer owners, possibly being divided at times, until by 1930 it was split into cottages housing workers at nearby farms and market gardens. Like many buildings that followed this downward spiral of occupation it has been demolished, probably when the cost of maintenance far out weighed the income from rents.

▲ After the Great War there was concern to provide council housing for working men. There was government aid and subsidies for councils to enable them to build as many as possible. The houses erected by Devizes Rural District Council are all built to the same design and are instantly recognisable in a large number of villages. The history of these 12 on the Devizes Road at Rowde is rather chequered. They were first proposed in July 1919 and later the 2 acres of land needed was bought from Lord Roundway for £150. However, the builders' tenders for the houses were considered much too high by the Ministry; it had been anticipated that each house would cost about £500 but the tenders ranged from £1000 to £1250. The matter dragged on for some years with disputes over architect's and surveyor's fees as well, but by 1926 the first of these houses was built at a cost of nearly £1200 each. Large numbers of rural council houses were built in the 1920s providing much needed modern accommodation for the men who had returned from the war.

Countrymen and Countrywomen

BUT WHAT of the figures that peopled this landscape? Many of those who were young men and women in the 1920s still live in Wiltshire, but the older well known characters have gone and the garden gate or pub inglenook will not see their like again. In general people were more self reliant than we would expect today and if help were needed it was normally no further away than your next door neighbour. In terms of material possessions and household gadgets a 1920s country cottage might seem poor to modern eyes but whether we are happier than those cottagers must be left to individual judgement of inherited memory or knowledge.

Most countrymen could perform a variety of jobs and some followed the calling of odd job men. A bit of thatching, carpentry, rabbit snaring, growing vegetables and helping at harvest would keep a man in the necessities of life. Other men who held regular employment could turn their hand to many things and managed to maintain their homes and gardens on relatively low wages while ensuring that there was fresh meat, eggs and vegetables when required. Clothes, though maybe old and out of fashion, were of good cloth, designed to stand a great deal of wear and tear and extremes of climate. The farmer and his family would be fitted out by tailors in the local town and often bought locally made boots and shoes that were created for the individual.

The village community was a varied collection of individuals. Farmers and farmhands predominated but by this time there would be some people who worked in a nearby town, though preferring to live in the country. There were still some craftsmen who had either learned the work from their father or been apprenticed when a youth. The gentry and the professions were nearly always represented and there were some poeple who had retired, often from the armed forces, into the country. The following pictures though show the men and women who really worked in and for the country – the farmer, his wife and the farmworker – and by whose efforts the Wiltshire landscape has been fashioned into its familiar pattern of fields, hedgerows, spinneys and woods.

Of the young people who stayed in the country the boys often followed their fathers on to the farm or into a trade. Many farmers' sons went to Lackham College of Agriculture but on returning to the farm still needed to prove their practical abilities to the older workers. At this time, however, more and more young men were moving to factories in the town. The choice for girls was less varied. Farmers' daughters often stayed to help out at home until they were married. In families where a regular wage from each adult member was necessary a daughter entered into service at one of the nearby big houses. The Great War brought about a situation where women could work regularly on the land but it was not until the Second World War that this became at all common. Opportunities for girls to work in towns were also fewer although there was employment to be found in the woollen mills of the western towns. For those of both sexes who had been fortunate enough to receive a good education the openings for careers were naturally much greater.

Most villages had stock characters whose names would alter but who stood in direct line to figures observed by Shakespeare and Chaucer. Men whose appetites for food, drink and lechery had passed into local legend and eccentrics whose exploits amazed their neighbours. Strange mystical beings who lived on the fringes of the community, or in the woods, and who in earlier centuries would have been in danger of being burned at the stake but who now made beneficial potions of herbs and could cure warts when doctors couldn't. And always a sprinkling of ne'er do wells and poachers. Many countrymen took the opportunity to come by a rabbit, hare or pheasant unobserved but the true poacher often poached as much for the excitement as for the pot. For him the thrill lay in the possibility of the hunter being turned into the hunted and for this reason he often eschewed a day's legal shooting.

Other figures made brief appearances on this landscape. Often they came from the town; doctor, vetinary surgeon, lawyer, auctioneer and tradesman. Sometimes they appeared from an even more rural way of life when gypsies or travellers made seasonal visits to work at harvest time. A growing number of tourists were appreciating the beauties of the English countryside and visited the better known villages and sights in the holiday season, giving the locals the opportunity for both conversation and profit.

The countryman, or woman, of this time then was self reliant, fairly contented and accustomed to both personal adversity and hard weather. They had often raised a large family, some of whom were educated at the local grammar school, and many of whom would no longer work the land. The old countryman of this time was the final flowering of a stock which went back to the time of Chaucer; someone who would moan about the little inconveniences of life but who would accept the greater machinations of fate with resignation. These pictures show the faces of people who belonged to the land rather than feeling the land belonged to them.

▲ It seems likely that grandfather and grandson ride in the cart pulled by a slow plodding Shire horse on a sunny morning in Keevil. A feature of family life in the country could be the greater influence exercised by grandparents who often lived near the families of their own children. Children could always be sent to granny at busy times when doubtless they were a little spoiled and were able to enjoy the freedom of a large garden with its succulent fruits. The cart is passing Pyatt's Corner, a fine timber-framed house, once symmetrical but later extended to the right, which unfortunately has been recently demolished.

85

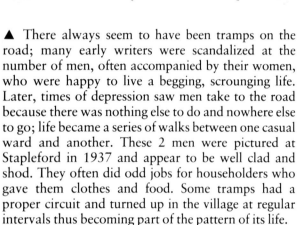

▲ There always seem to have been tramps on the road; many early writers were scandalized at the number of men, often accompanied by their women, who were happy to live a begging, scrounging life. Later, times of depression saw men take to the road because there was nothing else to do and nowhere else to go; life became a series of walks between one casual ward and another. These 2 men were pictured at Stapleford in 1937 and appear to be well clad and shod. They often did odd jobs for householders who gave them clothes and food. Some tramps had a proper circuit and turned up in the village at regular intervals thus becoming part of the pattern of its life.

▲ An unending occupation for the countrywoman was gathering wood. Mrs. Smart of Urchfont is seen 'sticking', probably collecting hedgerow branches for supporting peas and beans. The other task was 'ooding' which was the gathering of all dry timber for the fire. When ranges were used for cooking this was a year long job and whenever any member of the family went out they were expected to bring back some wood. Many of the older women kept old perambulators for this and were frequently to be seen pushing these piled high with sticks and branches.

▲ Owning no hearth, paying no taxes, the gypsies were the wandering roving people who the countrymen feared, distrusted, despised and sometimes secretly envied. Gypsy families travelled according to the seasons and were as set in their pattern of migration as the birds; gathering wood for making clothes pegs and baskets, picking flowers to sell in the town, hiring out their labour at harvest time and then retiring to secure winter quarters. At this time gypsies were sharply divided into those who travelled the roads as had always been the custom and those who had settled near towns and taken to dealing in scrap metal; both sides tended to look down on the other. When the gypsies were encamped nearby nearly any crime from missing hens to sick cattle was ascribed to them and they certainly made depredations into hedgerows and woods to keep their cooking fires burning. This gypsy, whittling wood to make clothes pegs, is camped near All Cannings. His wagon of course was horse drawn, for the great pleasure of the gypsy's life was horses. Breeding, buying, selling and extolling the virtues of his ponies was his greatest joy and ownership of a particularly fine horse would confer high status.

▲ In 1939 the Wilson family were encamped at Etchilhampton. Mrs. Wilson is pictured with her 6 attractive young children. The 2 on the right are enthusiastic models but the 3 to the left are a little shyer while the baby is definitely having nothing to do with the photographer. From the pile of material to the left of the trailer it seems that the Wilsons were dealers in scrap metal, making their living from what reckless countrymen threw away or sold as waste.

▲ Robert Crook of The Green, Urchfont, stands in his garden with mattock in hand in 1931. The mattock was a most useful tool being used for breaking up stony or hard ground, cracking tree roots, and scalping matted undergrowth from the surface of the ground. It was also a good trenching and ditching implement.

▲ Robert Crook again, later in life when he was aged 92 and dressed in his gardening clothes. His fitness is evident from the fact that he seems to be setting off for a day's work on his allotment. The wicker basket was doubtless carried home at the day's end filled with 'taters' or any other crop that was in season. After retiring from paid work many countrymen would meticulously tend a large vegetable garden or allotment providing a good supply of fresh vegetables to help eke out the pension. Very often a pig or a few hens were kept and fed on the waste vegetables.

▲ John Willis of The Green, Urchfont, in 1931. Mr. Willis is a woodman and is pictured among the trees that he tended. We forget that trees are also crops because they take many decades if not centuries to mature. Some woodland, however, was coppiced every 6 to 9 years when good crops of long stout poles were harvested. The men who worked in the wood were often philosophical and, encouraged by the living examples all around them, took a long overall view of life's problems. Much of forestry involved little contact with other men, except at times of felling and hauling, and the woodman was a very self contained individual.

▲ Many parishes still had a roadman who was responsible for filling potholes and maintaining the roads in a usable condition. He also kept them clear of mud and leaves and probably ensured that water could drain away quickly from the surface. To fill potholes he needed to break up stones into small pieces that could be tightly packed and tamped in to provide a solid surface. In 1931 Tom Gillett of Knowle was the roadman in Urchfont.

▲ Carrying his scythe out to the cornfields in 1939 is Mr. Wheeler of Great Cheverell. It is very unlikely that he would have used it in earnest on the corn and most likely that he was posed in a suitable setting. It is possible that he might have done some reaping with it in his youth but its normal use would have been for cutting grass, especially roadside verges, churchyards and orchards.

▲ With both open fires and ranges needing wood, men needed to know how to wield an axe to split logs to suitable sizes. This splendidly bearded gentleman, at Wedhampton in 1932, is the owner of a well-honed axe that has seen a great deal of service. Logs were collected, cut and stacked during the good weather and by the beginning of the winter cottages had a good wood pile to see them through the cold winter.

◀ Michael Ferris of The Green, Urchfont, with his horse team in 1932. The leather strap lying along the back of the nearest horse is the crupper, used for keeping the heavy collar in place.

▲ Charles Harris lived at Uphill in Urchfont in 1932 when he was photographed. He worked as a farm labourer and is pictured on pasture land against his everyday backdrop of fields, hedges and trees.

▲ The camera has caught Isaac Giddings with his eyes closed, as it has done with so many people both before and since. Isaac was a shepherd who lived at The Green, Urchfont, in 1932 and would have worked in the hills surrounding the village.

▲ Two splendid country characters, Mr. and Mrs. Bull, are pictured in a meadow at Etchilhampton in 1939. It is difficult to tell if the right hand structure in the background is a wheel-less wooden caravan or one of the redundant pieces of railway rolling stock that so frequently turn up in fields and serve a wide variety of purposes.

▲ Herbert Ferris of The Green, Urchfont, pauses with his fork in 1932. Indications are that it was a cold day as Mr. Ferris is wearing not only his muffler but also a Fair Isle pullover on top of his waistcoat.

Index